Praise for
Living on Islands
Not Found on Maps

Reading Luivette Resto's *Living on Islands Not Found on Maps* was like sitting down with my best women friends over coffee or wine, body loose, sharing stories of love and heartbreak, memory and family, pain and loss. With absolute candor, Resto writes about the whole range of being the woman she is: daughter, mother, lover, poet, dreamer, and Wonder Woman: "Her fans don't know about.../the bruises on her wrists/from deflecting bullets with gold bracelets,/and the calluses left on palms after lassoing lying kingpins." These poems trade stories until strength becomes vulnerability and vulnerability becomes strength, and we are all restored enough to venture back into the world and all its challenges.

—**ire'ne lara silva**, author of *Blood Sugar Canto*
and *Cuicacalli/House of Song*

Luivette Resto's poems celebrate the brujas, raised eyebrows, promised coffee, burn scars, and the language of the moon that we encounter in our daily rituals. Like the hungry tides, this collection challenges the colonized tongue. It beautifully wields sacrifice, humor, and power. From Puerto Rico, to the Bronx, to LA, and to all the uncharted islands in the sea, this is a journey filled with uncharted depths and possibilities, which we find "embedded here / in the pores and cells."

—**Juan J. Morales**, author of *The Handyman's Guide to End Times*

Poets travel with their minds, with their memory going places that only they can find. This is what is felt when reading *Living on Islands Not Found on Maps* by Luivette Resto. Memories of a difficult childhood to adulthood in the Bronx and beyond, these poems express Resto's ability to explore ability to use her imagination to enter and exit those unmappable islands. Spirituality, sexuality, motherhood, daughterhood, trauma, and healing are her themes as she moves in and out of memory and claims her measure of fullness as poet, mother, educator, lover, believer, and citizen, who is "trapping memories in a circle of fire and music" and letting us travel with her onto those islands, or out to sea.

—**Patricia Spears Jones**, author of *A Lucent Fire:*
New & Selected Poems

I'm mesmerized by Luivette Resto's hechizos y encantamientos--her poems are prayers from a deep and subtle marrow.

—**Luis J. Rodriguez**, author of *Always Running* and
founding editor of Tia Chucha Press

Living on Islands
Not Found on Maps

FLOWERSONG
PRESS

poems by

Luivette Resto

FLOWERSONG
PRESS

FlowerSong Press
Copyright © 2022 by Luivette Resto
ISBN: 978-1-953447-13-5
Library of Congress Control Number: 2022933420

Published by FlowerSong Press
in the United States of America.
www.flowersongpress.com

Cover Art and Design by Jasmine Preciado
Set in Adobe Garamond Pro

NOTICE: SCHOOLS AND BUSINESSES
FlowerSong Press offers copies of this book at quantity discount with bulk
purchase for educational, business, or sales promotional use. For information,
please email the Publisher at info@flowersongpress.com.

Dedicated to my Revolutionaries

Acknowledgements

These poems have appeared in the following publications, to whose editors grateful acknowledgment is made:

The Acentos Review: "Yemaya's Pantoum"; "This City Is Afraid of Me"

Altadena Poetry Review 2015: "Ode to Menudo"; "Like Mother, Like Daughter"

Altadena Poetry Review 2016: "Five O'Clock Shadow"; "last night"

Angel City Review: "A Poem for the Cunt on My Couch"

Anomaly #29: "La Coqueta"

Aster(ix) Journal: "The Legendary Legs of the Rodriguez Women"; "Solitary Encounters"; "A BX Love Letter"

bozalta: "My Love Is a Continent"

Chicana/Latina Studies: The Journal of Mujeres Activas en Letras y Cambio Social (Fall 2015): "Diana's Elegy"; "Painted Walls"; "The Legendary Legs of the Rodriguez Women"

COGzine: "Playing House"; "Botswana, Beats, and Bushmen"

Coiled Serpent: Poets Arising from the Cultural Quakes and Shifts of Los Angeles: "A Villanelle for the Kind of Woman"

Cultural Weekly: "A Poem for the Man Who Asked Me: Where Are Your Motherhood Poems?"

Dryland Issue 10: "A Letter to Gus, the Judgmental CVS Clerk"

Entropy Magazine: "Heirlooms"; "Like Mother, Like Daughter"; "Someone's Mom"

GATHERING: A Women Who Submit Anthology: "Promises Are Cofffee"

La Libreta: "All Day Every Day"

Lullaby of Teeth: An Anthology of Southern California Poetry: "John Hughes Does This with Spotlights"; "Breakfast Conversation with My Oldest Son"; "Unrecognizable"

Luna Luna Magazine: "Today Another Woman Painted My Daughter's Nails"; "The Lovelorn Astronomer"

¡Manteca!: an anthology of Afro-Latin@ Poets: "The Legendary Legs of the Rodriguez Women"; "Painted Walls"; "Garcia Folklore"; "Solitary Encounters"

North American Review: "Didactic #8: How to Exit a Room"

Pilgrimage Magazine: "A Garden of Paintbrushes"

Queen Mob's Teahouse: "Scars"; "The Canon"

Reforma Fall 2019: "MILF"

Revista Canaria de Estudios Ingleses, 2020, n.81: "Nomenclature"; "A Villanelle for the Kind of Woman"; "Vinculum"

Spillway 29: "Intimate Grammar Rule"

University of Arizona, The Poetry Center: "Living on Islands Not Found on Maps"

Upworthy.com: "The Case of My Resting Bitch Face (R.B.F.)"

What Saves Us: Poems of Empathy and Outrage in the Age of Trump: "Breakfast Conversation with My Oldest Son"; "A Poem for the Man Who Asked Me: Where Are Your Motherhood Poems?"

X LA poets: "My Love Is a Continent"

Table of Contents

Section One

Section Two

section one

A Boricua is born from the roots up
to study the light of the universe
the Earth's drum imbuing feet
with rhythms only the wind can carry.

—Naomi Ayala
"This Being the Last Tree"

Yemaya's Pantoum

When I visited the ocean
she told me
I was strong as her currents,
unpredictable like the tides.

She told me
brujas on blood moon nights
unpredictable like the tides
gather by her recursive feet

with a hand full of silver coins because brujas
know how to worship her coastline like an altar
and stand by her recursive feet
as the Perigean spring tide allows a kiss.

To worship her coastline like an altar
full of intention while gray waves move
like a plena as the tide allows a kiss
entropically move from me to you.

With full intention, waves glide
across our feet as her answers
whisper from me to you
strong as her currents.

Heirlooms

I didn't inherit everything from my mother.
Never runner-up of Miss Aguas Buenas
danced in white go-go boots
sang background with El Gran Combo
teased men with cascading, iron straight hair.
I inherited a temper, quick and malign.

I collected metaphors and similes like two dollar bills
while she created new wardrobes
out of self-drawn patterns and bargain bin fabric.

On February Sundays her fingers crocheted
baby blankets, scarves, matching hats and gloves
for the minus five wind chill factor.

She tried teaching me how to double stitch
but my holes were uneven like my voice
when I told her no for the first time.

I inherited a love for cooking tostones.
Her handwriting on an index card
instructs me when to turn the plantain over.

A monthly therapist bill became my heirloom
when her depression passed down to me
like diamond earrings.

Years later I would be expecting a daughter,
savoring the cotton of my sweater with my fingertips,
imagining my daughter's hair that soft
and what she'd inherit from me and her abuela.

My mother's thin smile looks back at me
when I see teenage pictures of myself,
the slight imperfection of her nose in a profile
reminiscent of the mother who abandoned her as a child
as I wonder about my mother's heirlooms.

The Legendary Legs of the Rodriguez Women

Unequivocal with his observation,
a New Orleans accent and a smile
the stranger comments, "Nice stems"
quickly passing by my shoulder,
creating a small breezy respite from the stale heat.

My cheeks responded in gratitude,
with thoughts of my mother
and the legendary legs of the Rodriguez women,
mythical like Ithaca and Helen.
The genetic heirlooms
from a grandmother I never knew
as 1970s pictures framed in sunflower yellow
document my mother standing on beauty pageant stages
in stilettos with an audience of wishful suitors
and envious women.

Instinctive like writing names on wet sand,
I touch the brown flesh and muscles below my knees,
wonder if Carmelita ever thinks of my mom or me
when she inspects the variant blues of veins,
slips on silk stockings, dances to Tito Puente,
wades in the water we call home.

Garcia Folklore

Located between the boundary of the Atlantic and Caribbean Ocean, a tide swept the two-year-old child commanding her body like an ancient sacrifice. The young mother disagreed, for the child had many lands to explore, stories to pen, books to read, hearts to collect, stories to learn. Swooping the breathless infant from the ocean's hands, she saved the child but the bones in the mother's back always remind her of the day she fought the ocean and won.

Like Mother, Like Daughter

The blend of Newports
and wine on my breath
remind me of my mother
as I light my next cigarette.

Holding it the way she does,
poised and lady-like
when she holds court during
unsanctioned smoke breaks.

Curve my left eyebrow like her
when I hear bullshit pick-up lines
or excuses masked as reasons,
talk with my hands
as I spew Spanish curses at
NASCAR worthy speed.

We hold our vulnerabilities
like we hold back our tears,
with purpose and protectiveness.

Smile when we really want
the earth to swallow us whole,
enjoy the silence of solitude
(a bit too much perhaps).

Dream to be a starfish because
like comic book heroes
they possess regenerative super powers.

Like the intersections of a Venn Diagram,
we share the shame of early pregnancies,

disgust for tolerated slaps to the face but
today I rewrite the plot of our lives
flicking ashes on the ground
knowing we will be them one day.

Nomenclature

Carmen is her name when I flashback to red handprints on my thighs for dropping a plate of rice and beans. It was Carmen's hair I pulled back over toilet bowls. Carmen's body I lay to sleep. Mamá wiped tears off my four-year-old face when the #42 bus never showed during a blizzard, and I had to miss kindergarten for the first time.

Luis is his name when asked, "Where does your father live?" and like a press secretary I reply, "He chose to stay on the island." His decision become confessions as we overlook the foliage of El Yunque. I see my face in his, silently hoping it is the only thing we share. Papá would have followed me like a character in a Tolkien novel, but Luis chose the women and vacilón over me.

Joseph is his name when I talk about his wife and other life across the George Washington Bridge. Joseph when my children and I are shooed away because how does he explain three brown nietos to white co-workers. Dad is the step-father who called me baby bear on Sunday morning phone calls, danced with me at my Sweet 16, gave me away at the altar.

Pseudonyms detach them from the people they are and the people I need them to be.

Someone's Mom

—for my revolutionaries

In my mind Don LaFontaine
narrates the beginning of every morning:
"In a world full of dentist appointments, field trips,
asses to wipe, lunches to pack, homework to sign,
one woman's name echoes through Rocky Mountain
laundry piles of Angry Bird underoos and Hello Kitty jeans,
one woman answers to the call of mommy."

A technicolor of communist color dresses,
Yankee caps, Converse sneakers, and
one faded "I hate people" t-shirt
proudly worn at PTA functions and children's museums,
occupy the closet where nothing pastel or animal print is welcomed.

Morning dance breaks to the Beastie Boys are mandatory
like syrup on blueberry pancakes
with a bacon smile and whip cream eyes.
A mid-afternoon glass from my favorite bottle of wine
in a sippy cup with the words "Mommy juice. Don't touch."
Sound like a Dora the Explorer episode
asking for things in two different languages.
Say darn when I stub my toe,
but scream motherfucker
when another parent cuts me off
at the drop off lane.

I pretend to change my name to Queen Sheeba of the Desert
plugging my ears from three voices and monsoon of questions.

How I wish to respond,
"No, I don't know why ants are that small
and who cares they are ants. Forget them.
Watch me take advantage of their size with this chancla.
Darwinism at its best."

On Columbus Day
I teach them about hubris, genocide and
respect for the property of others.
On New Year's Eve
write each of them a letter of the obstacles they conquered,
new games they mastered, colors they discovered,
the lines they stayed in, the boxes they thought out of,
new lessons they learned in and out of the classroom
like opening the door for anyone or the power of listening
especially when a grandparent speaks.

With each passing year,
in the surreal lands of Márquez and Paz
I challenge patterns etched in the knots of our family tree,
carve new ones in the extended branches
with smiles instead of tears,
hugs instead of raised hands and voices,
break traditions of alcoholism and apathy
with Lego hammers.

Take them to bookstores, show them
mommy's name on a spine so they know
guidance counselors can be wrong and
how anything is possible.

All Day Every Day

The Bronx isn't a résumé builder. You don't get a Scouts badge because you lived there today or 20 years ago. You don't come from the Bronx. The Bronx comes from you. And you don't survive the Bronx. It isn't trying to kill you so you can justify leaving it behind. Abandoning it like one of the buildings from the '80s with painted flower pots on the windows, making them more aesthetically pleasing for the Jersey commuters as they crawl on the Cross Bronx Expressway, which is always under construction. The Bronx is more than switching your *t*'s for *d*'s when you say water. The accent isn't part of your audition for the next Spike Lee movie. The Bronx is more than dancing to hip-hop and bomba. It's Lisa Lisa & the Cult Jam and TKA in the community center basement at your cousin's sweet 16. It's having enough spray cans and D batteries. The Bronx is the way your head tilts when someone says something suspicious. It is in the amount of *yo's* and *dead asses* used in a story. Because yo I am dead ass when I tell you that shit happened like I said it did. But in the end, we good. The Bronx is the original Yankee Stadium and hating on the Mets in perpetuity. It is witnessing love triangles at the park unravel like a telenovela. The Bronx is the ineptitude of the 2 train and cursing Robert Moses when you surface. The Bronx is knowing bodega aisles like treasure maps. It is getting ready for a night out, searching for your favorite hoop earrings and Boricua red lipstick. It means rolling without hesitation when your comadre hits you up. The Bronx is sitting at a faculty meeting and asking the questions no one is willing to ask because in the BX there is no sugarcoating.

Breakfast Conversation with My Oldest Son

Another man shot today, Mom.
I don't think I ever want a license.

Driving isn't the problem, Mijo.
Driving isn't the problem.

Didactic #4: Inspiration

With midnight in her eyes,
a blues song penned in Nashville,
sung in Ohio, whistled in Los Angeles,

inspired from the colony of white strands on her head,
the quixotic moments she thought why not,
said never again, and dreamed hell yes.

Scars

are reminders of survival
like the two dark marks between
my index and middle finger
left over from chain smoking Saturdays
when I ponder the existence of God,
cancer, the importance of taxes, democracy,
Nutella, jeans, cotton underwear, public transportation,
the Pantone color wheel, simple words like happiness
or, no, a smile opening a face.

Diana's Elegy

—for Diana García

I never wanted to write you this kind of poem. I hoped to write you an ode, praising the taste of your rellenos de papa that no one else can make without them crumbling into hands like chalk, or the way strangers confused us for mother and daughter in the summer time. In your eyes I was always the precocious toddler, raising the volume of your stereo as you practiced shorthand for the next secretary exam. The result of baby babble, Tatán was your name instead of Tía or Titi. An only child with only one Tatán, who cursed best in limited English, you taught me the best way to serve a volleyball, exchanged off color Spanish jokes like a teenager, yelled my name across bodega aisles. I missed the last decade of your life not knowing it would be the last, and funeral collages become memories I had forgotten. I never wanted to write you this kind of poem. I thought I would have more time to write you an ode.

Botswana, Beats, & Bushmen

At the art exhibition
she overhears a conversation
between the curator and an art buyer
a clinical psychologist

who has returned from
her annual trip to Botswana
where the Bushmen extract trauma
from the body and spirit
with dance around a fire
warmer than blood.

The eavesdropper closes her eyes
and her feet move up and down
to an imaginary drumbeat

      ball to heel
      heel to ball
      ball to heel

memories of a father
forgetting to pick up his daughter
on a typical humid Sunday afternoon
the itchy blue taffeta dress
incubating the seeds of rage and resentment

      what man will love her
      if the first one in her life doesn't

memories of mom's car keys taken away
when she forgot she was the parent
after three rounds of Long Island Iced Teas.

The eavesdropper needed the beats of Botswana
created from the hands of healers
trapping memories in a circle of fire and music
where case studies don't exist.

Promises Are Coffee

It's Wednesday
and I ask my father
if he can mail me
two packages of coffee
from Puerto Rico.

My request is specific and desperate:
It has to be Café Crema.
Abuela worked for the company
until she retired in her late 40s.
In between meetings
she created my name on her desk pad.
I can't find this brand in the States.

I ask my father
and he quickly promises with a
Sí, sí por supuesto
and I reply with gratitude
like a daughter would
forgetting the cardless birthdays,
the chances I gave away like bendiciónes
at the end of a phone call
and the afternoons where I waited and waited
like a daughter would.

But today he promises coffee
knowing how much it means to me
and I believe him
like a daughter would
because this is the kind of coffee
that can only be found on the island
just like him.

Ode to Menudo

Not the slang term for money, the Spanish translation for often or the traditional Mexican hangover cure soup dish. I was part of Menudomania. Wore my I heart Menudo t-shirt and side ponytail as I waited in line to watch their movie, *Una Aventura Llamada Menudo*, in a claustrophobic new city called The Bronx. The Puerto Rican Menudo. Renee, Johnny, Xavier, Miguel, and Ricky before Martín. The original Latin boy band, gracing record covers with feathered hair and curly mullets, skin tight, blindly bright primary colored pleathered pants, satin shirts with plunging necklines, showing off a pectoral landscape of early pubescent chest hair stubble. I was home for eighty-three minutes listening to my native tongue on the silver screen with its inflections, intonations, and sing-song melodies. Eighty-three minutes of forgetting why I had to leave my classmates, cousins, and the sunrises off the mountainside of Aguas Buenas. Sang along to "A Volar" wishing I could hop on an air balloon ride back to the familiar.

A Garden of Paintbrushes

A palate of her favorite color: red
matching the scarf
that once was an apron,
that once was a flag,
that once was the sheet
wrapped around her stillborn's body.

A Villanelle for the Kind of Woman

I never took you for the kind of woman
to let others sip her gin,
allowing the unacceptable to happen.

Letters address me: tough vixen
while comadres stand like sirens with corridos that begin
Nunca te vi como el tipo de mujer

echoing hymns born from the breath of the feminine
who never adhere to discipline.
Allowing the unacceptable to happen

underneath a transatlantic sky, widen
by a thousand moons, still like a mannequin.
I never took you for the kind of woman

who gave up searching for her own heroine,
vibrant and memorable like tattoos on the skin,
allowing the unacceptable to happen.

Catholic verses brazen
and overlapping W's on the chest, remind with chagrin
I never took you for the kind of woman
allowing the unacceptable to happen.

The Case of My Resting Bitch Face (R.B.F.)

I don't smile all of the time
I sit still, emotionless
looking straight ahead
with purpose
and somewhere in the timeline
of the post-feminist movement
this has been dubbed
resting bitch face
as if bitches had time to rest
on the body parts of their choice
when choice has been
taken, given, teased, vetoed,
questioned, compromised.

I am called a bitch by my pothead neighbor,
the guy I eye behind discount sunglasses,
the teenage cashier for my wad of coupons.
All because I don't place my emotions
on display to be picked apart like a thesis defense.

Society tells me
I shouldn't be insulted
with the connotation of the word
that means strength, confidence, empowerment.

But I don't feel empowered or strong
like an Amazonian princess
because when *quit being a little bitch*
comes out of a man's mouth
it means to emasculate and degrade

his friend who has decided to behave
emotionally contradictory to his gender.

What's up my bitches?
a dictum when a person
enters a room is not the salutation
of kings and queens.

That's my bitch!
affirms my membership
into a sorority
I never joined.

The latest newsfeed article
coins my stoic visage as R.B.F.
and in those still moments I am
insular and pensive
and my face is all I have
helping me make sense of the
sadness, pain, anger,
and the devolution of language.

This City Is Afraid of Me

"The accumulated filth of all their sex and murder will foam
up about their waists and all the whores and politicians
will look up and shout 'Save us!'…and I'll look down and
whisper 'No.'" —Rorschach, *The Watchmen*

It doesn't know what to do with messy people like me, who drown in the filthy rivers of self-doubt. A butterfly stares at my thoughts silently granting me permission to bathe in my own tears, tasting the choices from my skin, revisiting stories in the crevices of my mind. I don't want to be saved. I whisper to it, let me sit here with my rightful denouement. Its wings stroke my face, convincing me the gutters are no place even for the messy, living in this faceless city. All of us are born to love.

An Ugly Fact

I woke up with wine-stained lips
and an ugly fact of life:

I'm in love with the belief
you love me in return.

Unrecognizable

Invisible hands wrap her face
momentarily erasing the crow's feet and laugh lines
left after only thirty-five years.
Tighter they pull
making her unrecognizable to herself,
the woman she vowed never to be—
beaten, cynical, guarded.

When did this happen
she asks the mirror,
hoping for a fairy tale response.
Likes ones read to little girls
who believed in white horses,
handsome princes, poisoned fruit.

Tanned flesh
covered in kisses by Helios,
narrates her story
like the left ring finger
broken during high school gym,
reminding her about the
fragility of the body
and marriage,
or the burn scar on her right knee,
consequence of a drunken college night.

For those privileged
to slowly peel surly graphic t-shirts,
and superhero socks from her body,
they discover a fish shaped birthmark,
poetry inspired tattoos, stretch marks
left as souvenirs from pregnancies.

The skin is the largest organ:
holder of truth, age, experiences,
gravity's punch line,
porous as it soaks in tears
like sandcastles greeted by the hungry tide.

Living on Islands Not Found on Maps

I live on an island not found on maps. Growing up in the shadows of one of the most popular surnames: García. I speak Spanish to my abuela on Sundays but rely on Google to help my children with their homework because the accent rules never stuck. *Stress or unstress? Penultimate syllable?* Took the paradoxical college course: Spanish for Bilinguals where every Tuesday Prof. Cruz de Jesús would shake his head with indignation at my use of the familiar tú versus usted. No me conoce, he said. He was right. He didn't know me and I didn't know him or the proper word for bus or orange juice. What I did know is summers in Puerto Rico, eating quenepas as relatives asked, ¿No entiendes lo que dijo tu primo? And my abuela defending my tongue. This tongue. Colonized not once but twice. Leaving me isolated at family reunions. Feeling inadequate for my inability to conjugate on command. Sounding out store front signs while riding the #42 bus on the way home from Kindergarten where I concentrated to understand Mrs. Farrell's lessons about the seasons. But I finally found a home between Bronx bodega aisles, code switching with my homegirls about how many times Juana beepeó that boy we saw standing in front of él building. This became the island where I belonged. Unfettered and absent of red pen corrections. Juana didn't care if I used the tú or the usted or if my yo was about me or an emphatic reaction to her crazy story. This island didn't care if I rolled my r's or ever got the purpose of vosotros. An island where our bodies translated feelings: pursed lips, a raised brow, an aggressive eye or neck roll. We were bilingual neologists, inventing new lands we could carry in our Timbs and bubble coats. Here, language, like us, wasn't disappointing or broken.

section two

Moon marked and touched by sun
my magic is unwritten
but when the sea turns back
it will leave my shape behind.

—Audre Lorde
"A Woman Speaks"

Vinculum

Noun
1. *Mathematics.* A horizontal line drawn over a group of
mathematical terms.
2. A bond signifying union or unity.

She didn't need an abacus
to remember the nights she feigned sleep
caressing the middle of the bed
where they placed their children
the first time home from the hospital.

She didn't need to count
the bras left scattered on the nightstand
like fallen petals from red peonies,
hoping he would notice the beauty of her body again.

She didn't need to read her daughter any more fairy tales
about Prince Charmings riding on white horses,
saving princesses from dark towers or fire breathing dragons,
without crying each time she saw the words,
"and they lived happily ever after."

She didn't need.
She wanted.

To be undressed slowly
as he unyieldingly stared at her eyes
with the same curiosity
when he asked about her unspoken dream
to see her last name in the card catalog.

She didn't need.
She wanted.

To believe in colorless promises
repetitive like a merry-go-round
hurtfully circling like silent responses
when she begged for him to feel anything and
to see reciprocity in his eyes
when she said *I love you.*

Unpaid Parking Ticket

She grew tired of staring at the reminder when he left his car overnight outside the other woman's home. She unfolded two twenties' and a five from the wallet he gave her, walked slowly to the clerk's window like they do in funeral processions, graduations, weddings and when asked if she wanted a receipt of her payment, she responded, "No, thank you," like the lady her mother, aunt, and grandmother raised.

Painted Walls

Possessed by hours of HGTV and self-help books
I paint over walls
> beach sand hues over red delicious
> memories embedded
> in the irregular shaped corners
> of my bedroom   sanctuary   office
> mommy's special timeout place
and years of masonry experience
continue as I build new façades
hallmarked with "est.-in-1978" bricks
based in shame, carried daily
like my unborn child.

Shame wrapped around me like a *sábana,*
worn like my mother's favorite perfume.
Her scent enmeshed with mine
as I inhale and exhale
the toxicity of childhood silence.

Eat, drink, sit and talk with shame
like the siblings I never had,
fuck it until I get love out of it.

Forget it ever existed
in the palms of an alcoholic mother
and bruises on four-year-old skin.

Forgive the wife in believing
she was the dirty bitch
he claimed with each slap to the face
and bruises on thirty-four-year-old skin.

Stare at shame in the mirror
figuring out how to let it go
like an offering
left on the doorstep
of the ocean.

MILF

She's the mother I'd like to forget
the mother I'd like to forgive
the mother I'd like to find.

As I have become
the mother others want to bed
and forget they found,
trying to forgive herself.

A Letter to Gus, the Judgmental CVS Clerk

Dear Gus,

I didn't need the extra look of judgment
or the five-page receipt when I bought my Plan B pill

Yes, I had sex.
No, I didn't use a condom.
Yes, I enjoyed it, and
yes, Gus, I will do it again and again and again.

I don't think male customers get the same discernment
when they buy the industrial pack of Trojans,
extra thin and lubricated for her pleasure.

I am tired of my body being examined and decided upon
by men who couldn't find a clitoris
even if Alexa, Siri, and Google joined forces in some GPS version of
Voltron.

So save your visual admonishments
for I am not your Latin Mary Magdalene
although I am sure I did shout God's name more than once.

You will not side eye me for fulfilling my sexual desires,
expressing my sensuality, savoring the taste of a man's touch,
satisfying my fantasies one orgasm at a time,
loving my body under my own terms.

Sincerely,
An Unapologetic Woman

Didactic #1: Music Appreciation

Play my body fervently
like an electric guitar solo in a rock ballad,

ensconce me with anticipation
from a kiss—a decade in the making.

The Canon

She never saw herself in him
except when they laughed
at the names of cities
they will never visit
Sheboygan, Humptulips, Wallula.

Or when they shared
the commonalities of intangible pain
never imagining the realities of elegies.

They'd recite favorite last lines
of poets absent from the canon:
Jackson, Ayala, de Burgos.

They'd write spontaneous odes
only in couplets.

Their cities I've never seen banking on pounding feet.
Eclipsed by enterprise and collapsing infrastructure.

Gentle evenings filled with polemics
about the magic number of revisions
it takes before a poem is deemed complete.

Five.
No, eight.
Maybe, three.
Four.
Yes, four.

Undeserving, he answered.

When she asked him the cliché question,
"What word best describes you?"

Guarded, her response.

Carefully, like a fortuneteller opening a palm,
he approached her ear
humming with his lips
stopping at her earlobe.

Perhaps the poets were right,
they murmured.

First Edition

She placed her head on his chest carefully listening to the reverberations of his answers like children pressing their ear on conch shells. With the tip of his tongue, he traced each of her tattoos between questions about past lovers and clumsy high school memories. They tried to label this ritual but no word had been invented to describe mutual revelations transposed in the hours when night and day are blurred, and kisses on the mouth feel exhilarating like opening to the first page.

Renaissance and Providence

Nothing moves women so much as the possibility of saving a man.
—Octavio Paz, "My Life with the Wave"

Stemmed from an ardent hug
like the wave who moved ahead of the others
and the scandalized star guiding her onto the footprintless beach
where no one is saved with storybook endings,
the Pacific Ocean ironically cleanses atheist feet
with the belief in renaissance and providence.

Succubus

He finds her in the yellow dresses of all the women he encounters, in the smell of day lilies blooming in June, in the whoosh of bed sheets. Shared glances with others remind him of the man he will never be. Before sleep, when the body vacillates between consciousness, she writes her name on his back with the ends of her hair, exaggerating each curve and dip of her signature.

A BX Love Letter

He welcomed her at innocence,
surrounded her with dystopian landscapes
filled with lullabies sung by fire engines,
car horns, and police sirens,

made sure her Buster Brown shoes
hopscotched safely from Tremont Avenue to Crotona Park,
never falling between the concrete chasms
left behind from salt poured on icy Januaries,

listening to his metropolitan lessons
of trusting no one, following her instincts
versus hackneyed island rhetoric, writing
ekphrasis poems from graffiti murals.

Perhaps he made her too tough
as her body grew into her attitude,
forming hermetically sealed domains,
technicolor emotions wrapped in pink bows

like the arsenal of birthday gifts he gave her each year,
such as strip someone naked in two languages,
stare down urban Goliaths with brown eyes warmer
than the sun she was born under.

But one day she left him for another,
one who recycled the recycled,
ran strawberry stands with a sign
"Take a box, leave $5. God bless."

Her intentions left him empty, concave
as he howled promises to tear down the Robert Moses statue,
allow guavas to grow in her hair,
become her muse once again.

Didactic #7: Make Anything into a Race

To ensure fairness
we bite into each other's fruit
to get things started

then our fingers race to see
who can unpeel a Clementine faster
leaving a single rind on the table

and our mouths become the finish line
rushing to feed each other the first slice.

Solitary Encounters

His intellect reminded me of Spanish Harlem,
unpretentious but resonating,
as he discussed the gentrification of boyhood memories,
the irony of Paine's title *Common Sense*,
coined the term déjà vu history
when another child disappears, a shooting becomes rudimentary,
a person beaten for kissing the wrong person.

His philosophy on how the world works
reminded me of The Bronx,
unafraid of who he offended
as he revealed why he carries a knife
wherever he goes, why he will never marry
a woman named after a cocktail,
and why provocation is sometimes necessary.

He doesn't remember the inappropriate joke
we simultaneously smiled at, our goodbye hug
awkward like undergraduate sex
when hands don't know where they should go,
or how I stared at him longer than I should.

John Hughes Does This with Spotlights

No unicorns or rainbows live and frolic in these stanzas.
This will not be a sonnet worthy of Neruda's praise
nor will there be verbally ironic couplets of
red cockscombs blossoming in rectory gardens.

There will be no reference to the exhilaration
of seeing him walk into the room
where a spotlight like in a John Hughes movie
magically appears highlighting the vulnerability of his eyes
and her voice mutes everyone else's
especially when she says his name
which never sounded more perfect until that moment
because it came out of her mouth.

No reference to the synesthetic anticipation
of her scent in the morning,
outlining his jaw with her fingertips,
sighing to each other, this is not love.

The Moon Like Language

Driving home last night, I saw the Waning Gibbous phase of the moon and almost called to share its color with you and how close it seemed to sit on my house. *It is crushing my roof.* I wanted to say in that playful voice we used under the covers in the morning when neither one of us wanted to get out of bed to face the realities of the world. But the moon, like language, doesn't belong to either one of us.

Intimate Grammar Rule:
Laugh Plus a Preposition

laugh with me when it starts to rain on our beach day / laugh without hesitation and order a second bottle of wine / laugh despite wanting to shut down / laugh versus arguing about last night's miscommunication / laugh about the stupid thing that one guy said that one time we went to that place / laugh to make me feel less alone / laugh after I defy gravity and trip going up the stairs / laugh alongside me walking on the outside of the street because that's what your grandfather taught you / laugh through the hardest months / laugh in spite of wanting to yell / laugh for our survival / laugh at me when I snort / laugh at the moments I interpretive dance Barry White's greatest hits while making breakfast / laugh as well as hold me / laugh between the awkward pauses / laugh than cry / laugh underneath the covers as we share bad dating stories / laugh until we cannot laugh anymore / laugh during sex because that shit is funny sometimes / laugh except for when you want to kiss me / laugh like when we first met / laugh above anything else

Didactic #9: To~Do List

To sleep on a champagne crescent moon
like a hammock

hum unwritten symphonies
as leaves discover the spectrum of color

respond to lost postcards with
"I wish I was there too with you"

explore the 10,000 nerve endings of your lips
with mine.

On the Sunnynook Bridge

I pack pictures, concert t-shirts,
moleskins, exotic food cookbooks
into Sharpie-labeled boxes
written in my serial killer penmanship
as you comment,
"You suffocate the *t*'s. They look like an *h*."

Kodak memories from our Paris trip
spill on the forest green rug
borrowed four years ago from the cousin
who remarked at Thanksgiving
about the yellow specks in your eyes.

It was on the Sunnynook Bridge
where we added our promise
to the organized chaos of padlocks.

You fed me black mission figs and questions:
what do you think of the name Francis,
does the sound of a xylophone make you want to tip toe,
can zephyrs feel different in the Caribbean.

We took a picture in front of our lock
first in our best zombie faces
then by ourselves.
You insisted I smile
because the unevenness of my bottom lip
made you smile.

You said a few delicate words
before we turned the lock and

threw the key into the river,
watching it float next to other promises
before ours sank.

Didactic #3: Preservation

Lock up incomplete birthday gifts
in shoeboxes labeled "one day"

play punch buggy with a child
overreact as you pretend his fists are anvils

when they graze the flesh of your arm
the same place she holds tightly

on horror movie nights or Pacific Northwest gray mornings
gently pulling you back to bed with one squeeze.

The Lovelorn Astronomer

After every heartbreak
my grandfather would recite
the tale of the lovelorn astronomer

where the man fell in love
with the moon
one November evening,
hypnotized by her glow
reflected on the concentric ripples
of the Hudson River.

He loved the moon
even when she hid
behind onyx clouds,
her beauty only a sliver
of light in the nautical fantasies of men.

He slept in the daytime
so he could be with her at night
to read her verses
written in a new language
created from haste, lust, agony,
promise and compromise.

Whispered secret memories
never revealed not even to he,
sang ballads to the constellations
he renamed for her,
constructed syzygies
to keep her company.

I want to feel like
the lovelorn astronomer
one day, Grandpa.

No, Mija,
you want to be
the moon.

Didactic #5: Teaching the Obstinate

He taught her romance
still thrives and not sequestered
in the cynical stanzas of poems
she burns after writing them.

Five O'clock Shadow

Sometimes by lunchtime, the initial salt and pepper of a Short-Boxed Beard or a Soul Patch emerge. Plotting its multi-faceted uses, he remembers the quiver of a woman's legs as his hands glide up and down the bristles. It didn't take until five for stubble to grow on his cheeks, round like the Mexican mother whose quiet smile he shared. The nicks on his neck remind him of the ghost of the German father who never taught him how to properly shave. "Teaching wasn't his thing, so much as leaving," he confesses slinging another six-pack of pale ale into the brown bag of his favorite 9am customer whose name he never asks. As the day and smell of fermentation grow, he daydreams about the Prohibition Era. Pouring whiskey advice into shot glasses while men he secretly wishes were his father call him affectionate monikers like sport and kid. Polishing a chestnut bar etched with his initials like teenage lovers who never want to forget their firsts.

Playing House

I set the table like it was ours,
with the Chinese take-out you brought,
poured unoaked Chardonnay in glasses
as we sipped and talked about our exhausting days.

I washed the dishes and goblets
as the word honey
wanted to spill out of my mouth like the delta
and your shoulders leaned
on the kitchen threshold
like they were holding up the house.

It wasn't my house or yours.
It was an out-of-town lesbian couples'
whose Frida Kahlo artwork
we wished we owned,
even made up a cute story
how we found it.

You came up behind me
kissed me by their bookcase
reviewing classics we've both read.

Tired like working couples,
we took a nap in their bed,
as my breathing pattern
changed against yours
pretending this was
our everyday life.

Didactic #6: Gift Giving

Flowers are ephemeral like promises
earrings purely contingent upon the day's outfit
dark chocolate always an option
as long as it isn't bought at CVS, 99¢ store,
or the fourth qualifying item for a discount.

Let's exchange our favorite books
discovering aloud the nascent of our passions
page
after
page
after
page.

Send me a cornucopia of Art Laboe dedications.
I want to be Rosita from Lancaster
dancing to "Try Me" in my kitchen
making me forget I never went to senior prom.

Sing—our karaoke best—in each other's ear
"If This World Were Mine"
swaying our bodies to a slow two step
as I wait for a dip kiss like the movies
just as Tammi and Marvin trail off
"you know I need you baby,
really really need you baby."

A Poem for the Cunt on My Couch

Like an interloper
you walked into my home
without invitation.

So I must ask:
were my sofas soft enough
or did you feel their springs
when you sat down
crossing your Nair enhanced legs?

Did you struggle choosing
from wine glasses
etched with the names of vineyards
and memories you will never know?

Did the bathroom smell
like the entrance to Bath & Body Works?
Did the dishwasher have enough Cascade
to remove your dollar store lipstick
stains from them?

Was my plasma TV big enough?
The surround sound AMC quality
as you giggled like a child
watching a Disney movie?

Were the wall decorations—
my college diploma, first publication,
paintings of Puerto Rican independentistas
a caricature from my spring break in London
to your satisfaction?

Quality control is important to me
on a scale of zero to ten
with zero being your return
to a Bros. Grimm inspired abyss
for the uninvited

how likely are you to come back?

Didactic #2: How To Fall in Love with an Atheist

Say nothing after he sneezes
just offer a tissue

steal kisses like candid photos
taken when morning and evening

overlap like bodies, hands, sins
and benediction on Sunday.

The Lost Episode of Diana Prince

But the times require that I give myself willingly and become a
wonder woman.
—Nikki Giovanni, "The Wonder Woman"

She has it together.
What is wrong with me?
I wish I was like her.

Phrases like these reverberate from the inner monologue
of female audiences sitting on love seats,
leaning on boyfriend pillows.
Superheroes make it look easy
but she felt fraudulent
like a forced smile.

Strong women aren't supposed to cry in the shower
letting water and tears merge,
from the barrage of insecurities
as problem solver, healer, defender.

Her fans don't know about her
passing out in the boots
after too much sangria and sleeping pills
or how heavy the crown feels
even after she takes it off,

the bruises on her wrists
from deflecting bullets with gold bracelets,
and the calluses left on palms after lassoing lying kingpins
instead of believing their apologies anymore.

But there are days,
oh there are days
when she wonders
about the difference between the words
invincible and strong,
deciding which one she will be that day.

La Coqueta

*from the word coquette: a woman who flirts lightheartedly with
men to win their admiration and affection; from the Spanish word:
a dressing table; a vanity*

Nestled in a red chestnut box
rain droplets carved out
so its contents can breathe
my wedding ring resides.

I hold it in my palm
like I did our children's feet
examining their diminutive size
knowing they wouldn't fit there one day.

Today the surface of my dresser, *coqueta*
as my abuela calls it,
is covered in rings I have bought
since I took off the gold promise of a twenty-four-year-old
etched with a heart and initials.

Rings from flea markets in New Orleans
wooden ones wielded from the oak bark of another man's house
copper ones with the petroglyph of el coquí burned on
ostentatious rings that glitter and shine in the sun and moonlight
Nordstrom Rack bargains that cover two of my fingers
knuckle busters my coworker calls them.

Always on my right hand
anything on the left feels clumsy like first dates
I collect rings like paramours and dalliances
pull them off my fingers and leave them on my *coqueta*

my hands are mine now.

My Love Is a Continent

My love is a continent, an unconquerable land absent of manifest destiny.
No man's footprints, fingerprints, or flags planted on this body.

My love is a continent, pray and leave me ofrendas de chicharrón y empanadas
with a Malta India & white candle.

My love is a continent compartmentalized by states named after my whims & lovers,
uncolonized by anyone's demands, romances, or persuasions.

My love is a continent historians have yet etched into books,
unnamed by the best etymologists.

My love is a continent, a sanctuary for women
un puerto para las malcriadas, chingonas, cabronas, jefas, y sin vergüenzas.

My love is a continent for all of the outliers & anomalies of this world,
the forgotten ones who live in the gray.

My love is a continent without longitude & latitude lines or vector points.
You will not find my love on a map or Thomas Guide.

My love is a continent legendary like the Pyramids, enigmatic like the Bermuda Triangle,
unexplainable like your need to visit it over & over again.

My love is a continent I never want to give away.
I want to hold it in my arms & shield it from the brutality of the sun.

May my love live uninhabited, uninhibited, for it can't ever
be damaged, bruised, or burned to the ground.

last night...

last night in a dream
we rode a bus to somewhere
you played the trumpet
and I wanted to be so
vulnerable like the notes

Today Another Woman Painted My Daughter's Nails

Today another woman painted my daughter's nails, metallic pink reflecting off seven-year-old hands once gripped my index finger as I fed her 1am meals, naturally tanned hands disappearing into my palm when I kiss them good night, hold onto mine as she climbs stairs. Today another woman decorated my daughter's nails with the first color to adorn her 17-inch body, fingertips held by another who never contributed to the creation of my daughter's perfect ten fingers, ten toes. Never wiped off tears and kissed skinned elbows when my daughter thought she was the Latina Evil Knievel, defiantly zooming down hills on her scooter screaming, "I can do it, Momma!" Today another woman painted my daughter's nails, but tomorrow I will paint her future with a rainbow of my learned lessons about strength that rises after a cry, the necessity to sing off key at least once a day, and trusting manicurists who offer more than just pink.

A Poem for the Man Who Asked Me:
Where Are Your Motherhood Poems?

He didn't have the predictable inquiries
do I write in Spanish more than English
do I italicize the Spanish words
or include a translation glossary at the back of the book

with an accusatory tone like a private investigator
out to solve the case of the missing poems
as if I purposely erased my kids' existence and memories
in some poetic version of witness protection

should I write more about the irony of never wanting to be a mother in the first place
while other girls talked about having babies and a husband after college
I spoke about wanting 80-hour work weeks,
burying myself in depositions

should I write more about the abortion I had at 22
find the appropriate simile for the feel of the vacuum in my cervix
how I made my future husband witness and hold my hand
while I sobbed on the exam table legs wide open
reminding me how I got there in the first place

I think about the women who cannot have children
the price tag of IVF the bureaucracy of adoption
the women who still have to prove to their tías, mothers,
sisters, other women that their worth isn't in the uterus

because my body's sole purpose
is to be a vessel of life and not sexual satisfaction
never contemplating the perfect metaphor for the best orgasm I ever had

I should be careful of slut shaming myself in my sonnets
when I say fucking versus making love
pussy versus vagina
dick versus manhood

so where are the motherhood poems in question
they are embedded here
in the pores and cells
of this poem that cannot wait to breathe

Didactic #8: How To Exit a Room

I don't want to just walk out of a room
I want to saunter away.
Sashay really.
Sway my hips with invisible saucy subtitles
reprimanding you for looking.

I want to leave a room like Tina Turner at the 1985 Grammy's
when she walked up the stairs during the last few bars of
"What's Love Got to Do with It"
her famous legs, shimmery red dress, and strut
answering the very question of the song.

I want an ounce of her confidence
as she turned away from the audience
not caring if they clapped or stood up
not waiting for validation of her talent.

Her naked back,
brown and vulnerable,
becomes mine as I exit a room
not caring, not waiting.

About the Author

Luivette Resto, a mother, teacher, poet, and Wonder Woman fanatic, was born in Aguas Buenas, Puerto Rico but proudly raised in the Bronx. Her two books of poetry *Unfinished Portrait* and *Ascension* have been published by Tía Chucha Press. Some of her latest work can be found on the University of Arizona's Poetry Center website, *Bozalta*, *Spillway*, and *North American Review*. This is her third collection of poetry and first publication with FlowerSong Press. She lives in the San Gabriel Valley with her three children aka her revolutionaries.

CPSIA information can be obtained
at www.ICGtesting.com
Printed in the USA
BVHW081740090522
636553BV00001B/75